ANIMALS ARE AMAZING

OWLS

BY VALERIE BODDEN

W
FRANKLIN WATTS
LONDON•SYDNEY

First published in the UK in 2013 by
Franklin Watts
338 Euston Road
London NW1 3BH

Franklin Watts Australia
Level 17/207 Kent Street
Sydney NSW 2000

First published by Creative Education,
an imprint of the Creative Company
Copyright © 2013 Creative Education
International copyright reserved in all countries.
No part of this book may be reproduced in any
form without written permission from the publisher.

ISBN 978 1 4451 1927 4
Dewey number: 598.9'7

A CIP catalogue record for this book is
available from the British Library.

Printed in China

Franklin Watts is a division of Hachette Children's
Books, an Hachette UK company
www.hachette.co.uk

Design and production by The Design Lab
Production by Chelsey Luther
Art direction by Rita Marshall

Photographs by Alamy (Peter Arnold, Inc.), Corbis
(Ron Austing/Frank Lane Picture Agency), Dreamstime
(Joye Ardyn Durham), Getty Images (Roy Toft, James
Warwick, Art Wolfe), iStockphoto (gary forsyth, Laura
Hart, Megan Lorenz, Frank van den Bergh), National
Geographic (JOHN BOOTH/National Geographic
My Shot, MICHAEL S. QUINTON), Shutterstock (Eric
Isselée), SuperStock (All Canada Photos)

CONTENTS

What are owls?

An owl is a **bird of prey**. There are more than 200 kinds of owl in the world. They are split into two families – barn owls and typical owls. All barn owls have a heart-shaped face. Typical owls come in many different shapes and sizes.

This is a barn owl. It has a heart-shaped face.

bird of prey a bird that hunts and eats other animals.

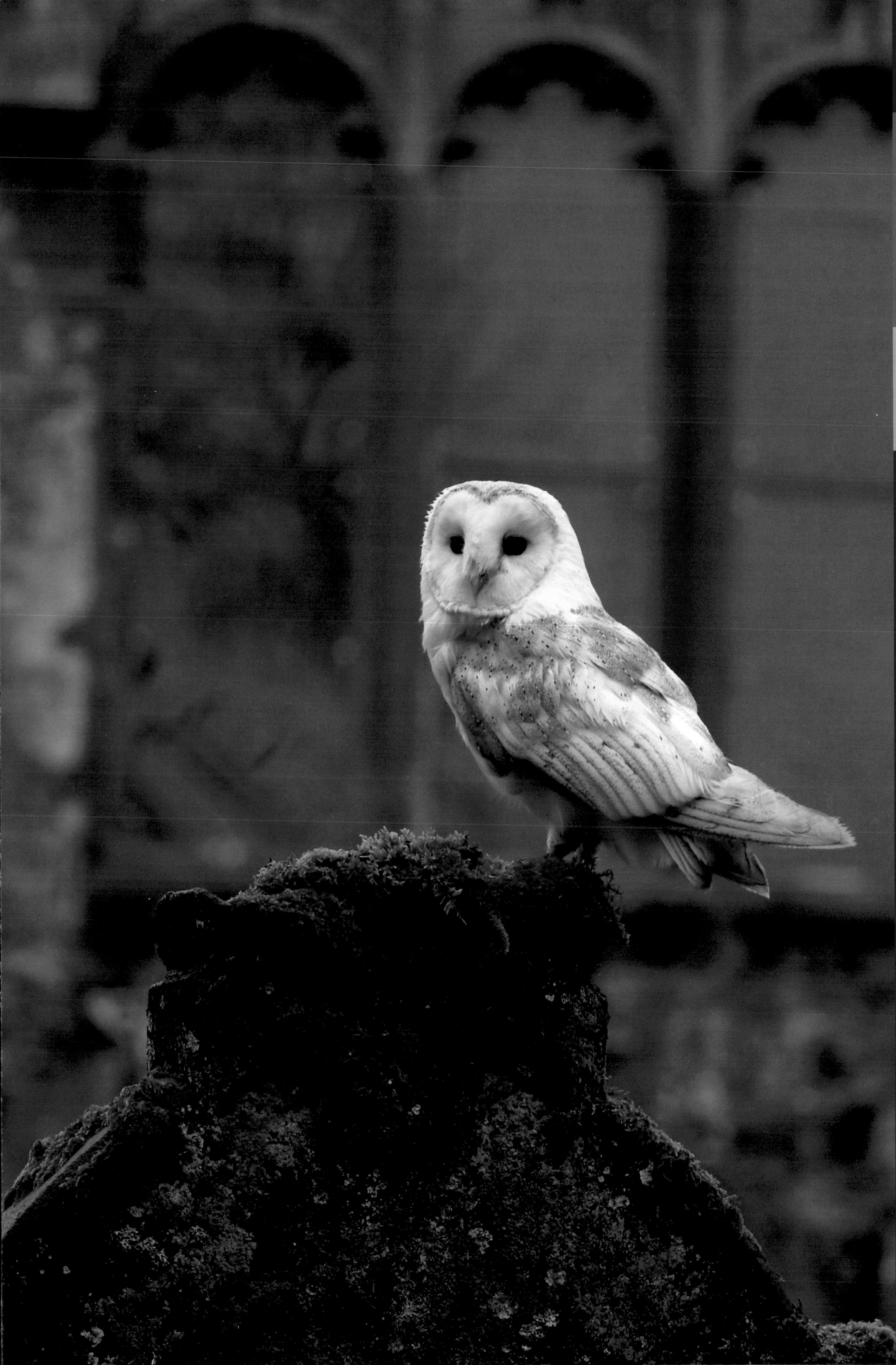

Feathery owls

Owls are covered with brown, grey, reddish or white feathers. The colours help **camouflage** them in forests so that they are not easily seen. Owls have a large head with big eyes and a hooked beak. They have long wings and sharp talons. Some owls also have large tufts of feathers that look like ears. These owls are called 'horned' or 'eared' owls.

The great horned owl has large ear tufts on its head.

camouflage a pattern on an animal's feathers, fur or skin that helps it to blend in with trees, bushes or grass.

Big owls, little owls

The smallest owl is the elf owl. It is less than 14 centimetres long. The biggest owls are the great grey owl and some types of eagle owl. They can weigh as much as a newborn human baby and be more that 70 centimetres long. Some owls' wings stretch more than 1.8 metres across!

The Eastern screech owl (above), which lives in North America, is much smaller than the great grey owl (opposite).

Where owls live

Owls live in every **continent** on Earth except for **Antarctica**. Some owls live in forests. Others live in dry, hot deserts or in grasslands. The snowy owl lives in cold, snowy places such as North America, Northern Asia and the **arctic**.

Some pygmy owls make nests inside desert plants called cacti.

continent one of Earth's seven big pieces of land.
Antarctica the continent that is also called the 'South Pole'.
arctic the cold and icy area around the 'North Pole'.

Owl food

Owls eat small animals such as mice. Some owls eat birds, fish or insects. Large owls will even eat rabbits or young foxes. Owls swallow their food without chewing it. Later, they spit out a pellet of feathers, fur and bones – the parts of their food that are not good to eat.

Adult owls catch food and bring it back to feed their young.

New owls

Female owls lay between two and twelve eggs at a time. When **owlets** hatch out of an egg, they are covered with soft feathers called down. Owlets leave their parents when they are one to five months old. Owlets have to watch out for larger birds that might eat them. Adult owls have few **predators**. They can live for 20 years in the wild.

Owlets lose their down feathers and grow adult feathers as they get older.

owlets baby owls.
predators animals that kill and eat other animals.

Hunting for food

Owls are deadly hunters because they can hear and see so well.

Most owls are nocturnal. This means they **roost** during the day and are active at night. They often sit quietly on a tree branch until they see or hear **prey**. Then they swoop down and catch it!

Most owls like to sleep during the day.

roost when birds sleep on a branch or perch it is called roosting.
prey animals that are killed and eaten by other animals.

Owl sounds

Owls can make many kinds of sounds. Some hoot. Others chirp, squawk, whistle or sing. They also make sounds by snapping their beaks and flapping their wings.

Owlets may chirp to get their parents' attention.

Owls and people

Owls can be hard to find in the wild because they sleep during the day. But some people watch them at night. Other people may set up boxes for owls to nest in. And many people see owls in zoos. It can be fun to see these nocturnal birds up-close!

These owls are camouflaged against this tree. This helps them to stay hidden while they sleep.

An owl story

Why do some owls have big eyes and long ear tufts? The **Native North Americans** tell a story about this. When the Creator made animals, he let them choose how they wanted to look. But they were not allowed to watch him make the other animals. Owl watched anyway which made the Creator cross. So he pulled hard on Owl's ear feathers and Owl's eyes grew big with fear. That is why many owls have large eyes and long ear tufts!

Native North Americans the first people to live in North America.

Useful information

Read More

British Animals: Owl by Stephen Savage (Wayland, 2010)

Learning About Life Cycles: The Life Cycle of an Owl
by Ruth Thomson (Wayland, 2011)

Websites

http://kids.nationalgeographic.com/kids/animals/creaturefeature/snowy-owl/
This site has facts, pictures, and videos of snowy owls.

http://www.rspb.org.uk
This site has factfiles on lots of different owls and recordings of
their calls.

http://www.barnowltrust.org.uk
This site has a kids area with lots of owl crafts, activities, games and
colouring pages.

Every effort has been made by the Publishers to ensure that these websites are suitable
for children, that they are of the highest educational value and that they contain no
inappropriate or offensive material. However, because of the nature of the Internet, it is
impossible to guarantee that the contents of these sites will not be altered. We strongly
advise that Internet access is supervised by a responsible adult.

Index